ELEANOR PARKE CUSTIS

GEORGE WASHINGTON

GEORGE WASHINGTON PARKE CUSTIS

WHERE WASHINGTON WALKED

RAYMOND BIAL

WALKER & COMPANY

NEW YORK

This book is respectfully dedicated to George Washington and all the brave men and women who first fought for freedom in the United States.
—R. B.

First published in the United States of America in 2004 by Walker Publishing Company, Inc.

Published simultaneously in Canada by Fitzhenry and Whiteside, Markham, Ontario L3R 4T8

Library of Congress Cataloging-in-Publication Data

Bial, Raymond.
Where Washington walked / Raymond Bial.
p. cm.
Includes bibliographical references (p.) and index.
ISBN 0-8027-8899-8 (hardcover) — ISBN 0-8027-8900-5 (reinforced)
1. Washington, George, 1732-1799—Homes and haunts.
2. Presidents—United States—Biography.
3. United States—History, Local. I. Title

E312.5.B53 2004
973.4'1'092—dc22
[B]
2004041931

Art Credits:
Art Resource, NY: pages 29 and 37
Brooklyn Historical Society: page 27
Mount Vernon Ladies' Association: endpaper images of Martha Washington, John Parke Custis, Martha Parke Custis, Eleanor Parke Custis, and George Washington Parke Custis; pages 21 and 35
N. Phelps Stokes Collection, New York Public Library: page 38
National Archives: page 26
National Portrait Gallery, Smithsonian Institution/Art Resource, NY: cover image of George Washington; page 41
Réunion des Musées Nationaux/Art Resource, NY: endpaper image of George Washington; pages 33 and 40
John Seder: pages 39, 42, and 43

For information about permission to reproduce selections from this book, write to Permissions, Walker & Company, 104 Fifth Avenue, New York, New York 10011

Book design by Diane Hobbing of Snap-Haus Graphics

Visit Walker & Company's Web site
at www.walkeryoungreaders.com

Printed in Hong Kong

10 9 8 7 6 5 4 3 2 1

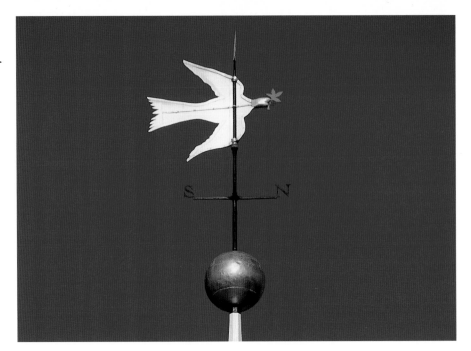

ACKNOWLEDGMENTS

I would like to express my deepest appreciation to the helpful and friendly staff at the following locations where the photographs for this book were made: Colonial Williamsburg, VA; Federal Hall National Memorial, New York, NY; Fort Necessity National Battlefield, Farmington, PA; Fraunces Tavern Museum, New York, NY; George Washington's Ferry Farm, Fredericksburg, VA; George Washington Birthplace National Monument, Washington's Birthplace, VA; Historic Fredericksburg, VA; Mary Washington House, Fredericksburg, VA; Mount Vernon, Virginia; Valley Forge National Historical Park, Valley Forge, PA; and Yorktown Victory Center, Yorktown, VA.

I would also like to thank my friend and fellow photographer John Seder, who made the photographs of Federal Hall and Fraunces Tavern, and the following organizations, which graciously supplied a number of historical illustrations for this book: Brooklyn Historical Society, Mount Vernon Ladies' Association, National Archives, New York Public Library.

I would especially like to thank Audra Acey and Dawn Bonner at the Mount Vernon Ladies' Association for their cheerful assistance with information and illustrations, and my editors, Emily Easton and Beth Marhoffer, for persevering with this book. As always, I would like to offer my deepest thanks to my wife, Linda, and my children, Anna, Sarah, and Luke for their inspiration.

George Washington was born on February 22, 1732, on a small plantation known as Pope's Creek in Westmoreland County, Virginia. At the time of his birth, no one in this rural colony could have predicted that this infant was destined to grow into a great leader—as the commander in chief of the Continental army during the American Revolution and as the first president of the United States from 1789 to 1797.

George was the oldest son of Augustine Washington, a Virginia planter, and his second wife, Mary Ball Washington. Augustine also had two sons from his first marriage, Lawrence and Augustine Jr., who were much older than George. Three generations of Washingtons had already lived here on plantations amid the woods and pastures.

In the mid-1720s, George's father built a home for his family on his tobacco plantation, known as Pope's Creek and later as Wakefield.

3

As a baby, George lay snug in a cradle that was
likely placed near his parents' bed in their home
at Pope's Creek on the Potomac River.

In 1736, when George was nearly four years old, his family moved about sixty miles farther up the Potomac River near Little Hunting Creek, which later became Mount Vernon. Two years later, his father moved the family to Ferry Farm near Fredericksburg, Virginia, to be closer to his ironworks in Accakeek Creek.

Along with three of his brothers and his sister Betty, George spent the next fifteen years of his life on this farm. Curiously, little is known about George's childhood—his image as a great man is so majestic that it seems he could never have been a boy. In 1852, the author Nathaniel Hawthorne noted that Washington seemed to have been "born with his clothes on and his hair powdered." Myths also came to be spun about his youth. In Parson Weems's fables, George supposedly chopped down one of his father's cherry trees and threw a stone (later a silver dollar) across the Rappahannock River at Ferry Farm.

George took his first steps on the plantation where his great-grandfather John, his grandfather Lawrence, and his father, Augustine, had lived.

Young George grew up at Ferry Farm, where he liked to roam the woods and fields around his home.

It is known that young George liked to explore the woods and fish in the river. He loved horses and became a skilled rider. Thomas Jefferson later considered him the greatest horseman of his age. He competed in athletics, which gave him strength and endurance when he later became a soldier. He enjoyed swimming, even though he was once quite embarrassed when, at age nineteen, two girls stole his clothes while he was skinny-dipping in the Rappahannock River.

Although his family was moderately wealthy as George grew up, the Washingtons faced hardship and pain. George's sister Mildred died in infancy in the fall of 1740. Just weeks later, on Christmas Eve, the family home burned, and the Washingtons took refuge in the nearby kitchen, which was separate from the main house. There they spent a dreary Christmas. The Washingtons rebuilt their house, but in early 1743, George's father died at the age of forty-nine, leaving his mother to care for him and his younger brothers and sister.

Ferry Farm was situated along the Rappahannock River, not far from the colonial city of Fredericksburg, Virginia.

In 1772, George purchased this comfortable home in Fredericksburg for his mother, who spent the last seventeen years of her life here.

The death of his father changed the course of young George's life. At eleven years old, he inherited Ferry Farm, although its income went to his mother. He later recalled, "All I am I owe to my mother. I attribute all my success in life to the moral, intellectual and physical education I received from her." A woman of independent spirit, Mary Ball Washington never remarried. With the help of overseer Edward Jones, she lived on the plantation until 1772, when George bought a house for her on Charles Street in nearby Fredericksburg.

During these years, George came to depend on his half-brother Lawrence, who lived at Mount Vernon. He deeply admired his likable, well-mannered brother, who had been educated in England. Fourteen years older than George, Lawrence had married into the Fairfax family. These prominent Virginians later helped launch George's career.

As a young man, George socialized with friends at taverns, such as the Rising Sun in Fredericksburg, which were popular gathering places in colonial America.

As a boy, George longed to go to sea, but his mother strongly discouraged him because of the hardships of a sailor's life. So, as he grew to manhood, he turned his adventurous nature toward the military arts and the settling of western lands. In 1748, he became a surveyor and, at the age of sixteen, received an appointment to survey the sprawling lands of Thomas, Lord Fairfax, in the Shenandoah Valley.

In 1752, George surveyed the land for the site of Kenmore Plantation, which his sister Betty and her husband, Colonel Fielding Lewis, built just before the Revolution.

Meanwhile, his brother Lawrence had become ill with tuberculosis, and George went with him to Barbados in hopes that he would be cured in the warm climate. The illness was too advanced, however, and Lawrence died in 1752, leaving George brokenhearted. After Lawrence's death, George inherited the Mount Vernon estate, and its many responsibilities left him with little time for grief.

In July 1752, George inherited the sprawling Mount Vernon plantation upon the death of his older brother Lawrence Washington.

In November 1754, Washington led the Virginia expedition to challenge French claims to
the Ohio River Valley located in the wilder-
ness of Pennsylvania.

George also became caught up in the growing rivalry between the British and French over control of the Ohio Valley. Young and ambitious, he wanted to distinguish himself as a military leader in the looming conflict. In October 1753, he was sent by Governor Robert Dinwiddie on a mission to warn the French commander at Fort Le Boeuf not to push into British-claimed territory. Although his mission failed, Washington gained a great deal of fame and admiration. After his return, his diary was published at Williamsburg, then the capital of Virginia. The diary, which vividly described the hardships and dangers of his journey, likely helped Washington earn a commission as lieutenant colonel in 1754, even though he was only twenty-two years old. Despite his youth and inexperience, Washington learned quickly and earned the respect of his superiors.

As part of his uniform, Washington wore a familiar tricornered hat, which distinguished him as a colonial officer.

In the spring of 1754, Washington led his Virginia forces through the dense forests in pursuit of the French at Fort Duquesne, in the upper Ohio River Valley.

14

The conflict between Great Britain and France soon led to the French and Indian War of 1754 to 1763 in which the two nations struggled for control of North America. As a colonial officer with a rank of lieutenant colonel, George Washington fought in the first skirmishes of this war. In early April 1854, he journeyed with the Virginia militia under Colonel Fry to establish a post at the Forks of the Ohio, the present site of Pittsburgh. Along the way, the militia learned that the French had already built Fort Duquesne there—and that a force of French soldiers and their Indian allies were advancing toward the British troops. On May 24, Washington ordered his men to encamp at Great Meadows, Pennsylvania. Although much of the meadow was a soggy marsh, Washington considered it "a charming field for an encounter."

While on a military campaign, colonial officers and soldiers camped in tents pitched on the open ground.

Three days later, the colonial militia heard that a group of French soldiers was about seven miles away. The militia ambushed the French, killing ten soldiers, including their commander. One French soldier was wounded and twenty-one men were captured. A French soldier managed to escape to carry news of the attack to Fort Duquesne. The colonials lost only one soldier and two were wounded, including their leader, Colonel Fry. When the colonel died at Wills Creek on May 31, Washington took command of the regiment and was promoted to colonel. Fearing "we might be attacked by considerable forces," he quickly had his men build Fort Necessity.

When he learned that the French and their Indian allies were advancing toward him, George hastily built Fort Necessity at Great Meadows, Pennsylvania.

16

Fort Necessity consisted of little more than a circular wall of upright logs. After defeating a French scouting party, Washington was later forced to surrender the fort after a short battle.

On the morning of July 3, 1754, a large force of six hundred French soldiers and one hundred Indians advanced on Fort Necessity and engaged the smaller colonial forces in a daylong battle in a drenching rain. Outnumbered and surrounded by enemy troops, with their food provisions nearly gone and their gunpowder wet and useless, Washington reluctantly surrendered. He was discouraged by this humiliating defeat, especially when he realized that, in the confusing language of the surrender terms, he had mistakenly agreed to apologize for the death of the French leader.

Washington was further angered by unfair differences in rank and pay between British and colonial officers, who were regarded as inferiors. Toward the end of 1754, he decided to leave the army. Still, in April of the following year he volunteered to join a British expedition against the French at Fort Duquesne as an aide to General Edward Braddock. On July 9 the British were ambushed by the French and their Indian allies on the Monongahela River. Washington had fallen seriously ill with "fevers and pains." He also had several near misses as four bullets ripped through his coat and two horses were shot from under him. Yet he heroically led the Virginia troops after Braddock was killed in battle. Braddock was widely criticized for his foolish decisions, which led to the British defeat. However, Washington was widely praised for his courageous and intelligent actions under fire.

This boulder marks the site of the Old Braddock Road, where the British general met his fate at the hands of French soldiers and native allies.

In 1755, at the young age of twenty-three, George Washington was appointed commander in chief of the Virginia militia, with responsibility for defending the 350-mile frontier. Over the next few years, he grew from a sometimes vain and impatient young soldier to a mature, intelligent officer with a solid understanding of military leadership and colonial politics.

As the British expedition advanced on Fort Duquesne, axmen struggled to cut a road through the dense forests of Pennsylvania.

Washington left the army in 1758 and returned to his home at Mount Vernon. For years, he had neglected the estate, but he now put up new buildings, refurnished the house, and experimented with new crops. Years before, he had been in love with a beautiful neighbor. However, when she married another, he realized that he must find a good wife for himself. He soon met Martha Dandridge Custis, the well-to-do young widow of Daniel Parke Custis. Martha fell in love with George, and he found her attractive. Her pleasant nature and wealth likely also appealed to him.

At the end of the French and Indian War, George Washington returned to his Mount Vernon home, which overlooked the Potomac River.

On January 6, 1759, he and Martha were married. He wrote to a friend, "I believe I have settled with an amiable wife for the remainder of my life and hope to find in my retirement more happiness than I have ever found in a large and troubled world." Throughout their long marriage, George and Martha would remain tenderly devoted to one another. George also became a loving father to Martha's young children, Martha (Patsy) and John Parke (Jacky). With the marriage, George immediately became one of the most prominent landowners in Virginia.

(Top) When George married Martha, he assumed the duties of a father to her children, Martha (Patsy) and John Parke (Jacky).

(Bottom) This painting by Junius Brutus Stearns depicts the marriage of George Washington and Martha Dandridge Custis, widow of Daniel Parke Custis, in 1759.

In 1859, Washington began fifteen years of service in the Virginia House of Burgesses, located in Williamsburg, where he often dined and attended balls at the Governor's Palace.

From this time until the outbreak of the American Revolution, he took care of his lands around Mount Vernon and gradually became involved in colonial politics. With the support of a growing circle of powerful friends, Washington came to serve in the Virginia House of Burgesses in Williamsburg from 1759 to 1774. During these years, he and Martha also experienced the tragedies and joys of family life. Patsy had an epileptic seizure and died in 1773 at the age of seventeen, leaving her parents devastated. Jacky met Eleanor (Nelly) Calvert, and they were married on February 3, 1774.

George Washington was a familiar figure on the streets of Williamsburg.

Washington also became actively involved in the growing discontent with Great Britain. At first he hoped the colonies would be able to settle their differences with the mother country, although he was still deeply offended that British officers had treated him and other colonial officers so badly. But after 1763, British restrictions frustrated Washington's plans for buying western lands. He also came to believe that British trade laws were unfair to colonial planters. As the quarrel with Great Britain worsened, he often spoke out against these unjust policies.

As a delegate to the First and Second Continental Congress in 1774 to 1775, Washington's calm, steady presence and outstanding military record inspired confidence in the other delegates. In June 1775, Congress unanimously chose George Washington as commander in chief of the Continental army.

(Left) Washington often attended services at Bruton Parish Church, along with Thomas Jefferson, Richard Henry Lee, Patrick Henry, George Mason, and other notable people.

On July 3, 1775, Washington left Mount Vernon and took command of the poorly trained and equipped troops at Cambridge, Massachusetts, near Boston, which was occupied by the British. He devoted himself to drilling the ragged fourteen-thousand-man army and trying to secure desperately needed gunpowder and other supplies. He said, "Discipline is the soul of an army. It makes small numbers formidable; procures success to the weak, and esteem to all."

While George was in Cambridge, Martha, Jacky, Nelly, and several friends journeyed two weeks to spend Christmas with him. The others then returned home, but Martha remained with George until June 1776.

After Washington was appointed commander in chief of the Continental army on June 15, 1775, he greeted forces from several colonies in Cambridge. These men became the foundation for his army.

Martha would not see her husband again until March 1777, at Morristown, New Jersey, where the army had camped for the winter. She came to nurse him back from an illness, but he sent her home when the fighting drew near.

Washington quickly realized that with his limited forces the best strategy would be to move cautiously against the British. Early in March 1776, George occupied Dorchester Heights. From this position, he effectively commanded the city and forced the British to withdraw on March 17. He then moved to defend New York City, but he made a serious mistake when he occupied a position in Brooklyn that could not be defended and lost New York City to the British. However, he was able to skillfully retreat from Manhattan into Westchester County and back through New Jersey into Pennsylvania.

As the British landed at Brooklyn on August 22, 1776, Washington knew that he confronted a large and powerful force of British soldiers.

In the last months of 1776, desperately short of men and supplies, Washington nearly despaired. The enlistment period was almost up for many of the troops, and others were deserting in droves. Fearing that the British might attack the capital in Philadelphia, Congress had even left the city.

In a daring move, Washington quietly crossed the Delaware River on Christmas night, 1776. In a brilliantly planned attack, he then surprised the garrison of hired German soldiers, known as Hessians, at Trenton, New Jersey. Washington advanced to Princeton, New Jersey, where he defeated the British on January 3, 1777. Colonial hopes were briefly revived. However, in September and October 1777, he suffered two defeats in Pennsylvania—at Brandywine and Germantown.

The one significant victory of that year came in October 1777, when the British were defeated at Saratoga, New York. However, Benedict Arnold and Horatio Gates—not George Washington—had led American forces in this battle. Because of Washington's string of defeats, some members of Congress and army officers tried to replace Washington with another commander. The scheme known as the Conway Cabal eventually failed because of Washington's popularity and his overall military superiority.

Entitled Washington Crossing the Delaware, *this painting by Emanuel Leutze portrays a leader undaunted by the task before him.*

Washington managed to hold together his tattered and discouraged army through the long, hard winter at Valley Forge. Along with two brilliant military leaders, the Prussian Baron von Steuben and the French Marquis de LaFayette, he shaped the army into an effective fighting force. By the spring of 1778, he believed that his army was ready to take the field again. In June, he attacked the British near Monmouth Courthouse, in New Jersey, as they withdrew from Philadelphia to New York. Washington's quick action on the field gave the Americans a badly needed victory.

(Top) During the long winter of 1777, Washington's troops took shelter in log cabins erected at Valley Forge.

(Right) Inside the dark, windowless cabins at Valley Forge, American soldiers endured many hardships, including hunger and cold.

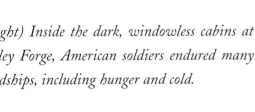

Over the course of the war, George Washington grew enormously in ability as a military leader. He gradually came to trust his own judgment on the battlefield. He learned to combine new, inexperienced troops with veterans to form effective fighting units. Often accused of being too cautious, he boldly changed plans and took risks when victory seemed possible. He also learned the art of diplomacy in dealing with state governments and Congress. This became one of his greatest strengths.

While wintering at Valley Forge, George Washington maintained his headquarters in this stately house.

This row of cannons at Yorktown illustrates the determination of George Washington to prevail in the war for American independence.

(Top right) Today, this monument overlooks the battleground at Yorktown, where George Washington at last triumphed over British military forces.

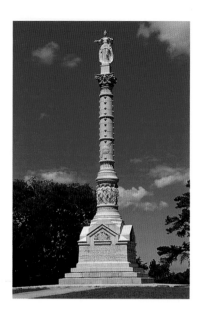

By 1780, the key battles of the war had shifted to the south. The campaigns in Virginia and the Carolinas were led by other generals, including Nathanael Greene and Daniel Morgan, but Washington remained in charge of the overall strategy of the war. That year, the French army arrived in Virginia, and Washington brought them into his overall war plans.

In 1781, he launched a cleverly planned and executed campaign against General Charles Cornwallis at Yorktown. On October 19, 1781, Cornwallis was forced to surrender his entire army. After the decisive victory of Yorktown, the American Revolution was over. However, the victory had to be bittersweet for Washington. Having grown restless at home, Jacky volunteered to become an aide for his stepfather. Just a few days after enlisting, he died of "camp fever" on November 5, 1781.

(Left) Siege of Yorktown *by Louis-Charles Auguste Couder depicts the decisive victory in the Revolutionary War.*

"I can really say I had rather be at home at Mount Vernon with a friend or two about me, than to be attended at the seat of the government by the officers of State and the representatives of every power in Europe."

34

Following his brilliant triumph in the war, George Washington returned home, where he could finally devote himself to his beloved Mount Vernon. After Jacky died, his wife, Eleanor Custis, remarried, and their children, Eleanor Parke (Nelly) Custis and George Washington Parke Custis, went to live with George and Martha. A cheerful and mischievous boy, young George, nicknamed "Wash" and "Tub," was very proud to have such a famous grandfather. After the boy recovered from an illness in 1784, his grandfather wrote that he was "as fat & saucy as ever." Bright and lovely Nelly, of whom the president was especially proud, later married George's favorite nephew, Lawrence Lewis.

(Left) After the death of Jacky, his daughter Nelly went to live with her grandparents, George and Martha, at Mount Vernon.

(Right) George Washington Parke Custis, brother of Nelly and stepgrandson of George Washington, also went to live at Mount Vernon after his father died.

35

During this time, Washington built a greenhouse, a mill, an icehouse, and added land to the estate. He experimented with crop rotation to improve soil fertility. He bred horses and hunting dogs. He explored the potential of the Potomac River for navigation and various other ventures. In his diary, he noted the many visitors—American and foreign—who streamed to Mount Vernon, which had quickly become a national institution.

Among the many improvements at Mount Vernon were these impressive barns, built by George Washington.

As much as he wished to remain at Mount Vernon, Washington realized that the United States government was not functioning well under the Articles of Confederation. So, he became a strong force in calling for a Constitutional Convention. In May 1787, Washington left Mount Vernon and led the Virginia delegation to the Constitutional Convention in Philadelphia. There he was unanimously elected presiding officer. Although he seldom spoke in meetings, he tended to support those in favor of a strong central government. More important, his very presence brought great prestige to the convention. After the new Constitution was sent to the states for ratification, George Washington was unanimously chosen by the Electoral College in 1789 as the first president of the United States.

The signing of the Constitution was one of the most important events in American history, after which George Washington became the first president of the United States.

On April 30, 1789, George Washington stood on the balcony of Federal Hall on Wall Street in New York, the national capital at that time, and took his oath of office as the first president of the United States. The president knew that he would have to act carefully and deliberately, as a model, because he was setting a standard for future presidents. He wrote to James Madison, "I walk on untrodden ground. There is scarcely any part of my conduct which may not here-after be drawn into precedent."

This engraving by Amos Doolittle after a drawing by Peter Lacour shows Washington taking the oath of office as president at Federal Hall in New York City.

Hoping to unite the states into a strong nation, Washington toured New England in 1789 and the South in 1791. A skilled administrator and able leader, he believed that "government is not reason, it is not eloquence, it is force; like a fire, a troublesome servant and a fearful master." Concerned about abuses of power, he stated, "Occupants of public offices love power and are prone to abuse it," and "Few men have virtue to withstand the highest bidder." He wisely left policy-making powers to Congress as the legislative branch but believed that foreign policy should primarily be an executive concern.

After Washington was inaugurated at Federal Hall on April 30, 1789, New York served as the country's first capital until it moved to Philadelphia in 1790.

Although he was a very skilled leader, Washington could not heal the deepening conflict between Secretary of State Thomas Jefferson and Secretary of the Treasury Alexander Hamilton. He supported many of Hamilton's controversial policies for a strong federal government. However, Jefferson and his followers believed in individual rights and greater independence for the states. Conflict between these two groups, the Hamiltonians and the Jeffersonians, led to the political party system.

During Washington's presidency, fellow Virginian and future president Thomas Jefferson championed the rights of individuals and the independence of state governments.

In 1792, Washington was reelected president, and the following year he faced the worst crisis of his administration. Members of his own cabinet argued heatedly over American participation in a major war between England and France triggered by the French Revolution. Washington wanted to stay out of the war, which angered the Jeffersonians, who wanted the United States to support France. However, Washington was horrified by the bloody excesses of the French Revolution, and he was enraged by French meddling in American politics. He also looked forward to profitable trade with the British in the future. So, he agreed with the Hamiltonians that the United States should maintain peace with Great Britain. In 1794, he accepted the Jay's Treaty, which settled a number of outstanding disputes between the United States and Great Britain. The Jeffersonians were shocked, viewing the treaty as giving in to British demands. They railed against the president for this action.

When Washington was president in the first years of the republic, Alexander Hamilton advocated a strong, unified federal government.

In New York City on December 4, 1783,
Washington bid farewell to his officers at
Fraunces Tavern, which later housed offices of
the Continental Congress.

Weary of politics and feeling old, Washington decided not to run for a third term, establishing a model that is followed to the present day. When George Washington left office in March 1797, he could list a number of notable accomplishments. The finances of the young nation were well established. Native American attacks on settlers east of the Mississippi had largely ended. Although he was disappointed that two distinct political parties had taken shape by the end of his first term, the two-party system has become an important strength of American politics.

Washington made a brilliant Farewell Address in which he urged his fellow Americans to shun party politics and regional distinctions in favor of national unity. In foreign affairs, he warned the United States against making long-term alliances abroad. He was succeeded by his vice president, John Adams, who believed in a strong federal government.

Fraunces Tavern in New York City has been restored and still may be visited by anyone interested in early American history.

FRAUNCES TAVERN

After the American Revolutionary War, on December 4, 1783, General George Washington bade an emotional farewell to his officers at a banquet held in the Long Room, located on the second floor of this tavern. Samuel Fraunces, a West Indian innkeeper, was the proprietor; he later became Washington's chief steward. Fraunces, also an American patriot, was host to secret meetings of the Sons of Liberty and gave aid to American prisoners of war. The present building, purchased by the Sons of the Revolution in 1904, was restored by them on this site and has since been maintained by them.

Plaque provided by the New York Community Trust, 1976

George Washington then went home to Mount Vernon to spend his last years in quiet retirement at his sprawling estate. Over the years, he and Martha had enjoyed a long and loving marriage. However, Washington had less than three pleasant years with Martha at Mount Vernon. In December 1799, he became ill with a throat infection, or acute laryngitis. As he quickly weakened, he said, "Doctor, I die hard, but I am not afraid to go."

As he slipped away at Mount Vernon on December 14, 1799, Washington's last words were, "I am just going. Have me decently buried and do not let my body be into a vault in less than two days after I am dead. Do you understand me . . . ? 'Tis well."

In his will, Washington stated that all his and the Custis slaves would be freed upon the death of Martha. In 1778, during the Revolution, he had come to view slavery as a great wrong, especially in a nation in which all people were created equal. He was the only slaveholding president to liberate his slaves. He arranged for the old and frail slaves to receive proper care for the rest of their lives and for the children to be taught to read and write.

For months after his death, the nation mourned the loss of their first president. And generations of Americans have since revered the great man who wisely and skillfully guided a young republic through its first uncertain years.

George, and later Martha, was buried at Mount Vernon. On the occasion of Washington's death, Henry Lee spoke of him, "First in War, first in peace, and first in the hearts of his countrymen, he was second to none in the humble and endearing scenes of private life."

SOURCES

Many of the following books were consulted in the research and writing of Where Washington Walked. *These books are recommended to anyone who would like to learn more about this impressive man.*

"I conceive that a knowledge of books is the basis on which all other knowledge rests."

—George Washington

Alden, John R. *George Washington: A Biography.* Baton Rouge: Louisiana State University Press, 1984.

Blackaby, Anita D. *Washington and the American Revolution: A Guide to the Campaigns in Pennsylvania & New Jersey.* Washington Crossing, PA: Council of American Revolutionary Sites, 1986.

Carp, E. Wayne. *To Starve the Army at Pleasure: Continental Army Administration and American Political Culture, 1775–1783.* Chapel Hill: University of North Carolina Press, 1984.

Dalzell, Robert F., Jr., and Lee Brown Dalzell. *George Washington's Mount Vernon: At Home in Revolutionary America.* New York: Oxford University Press, 1998.

Elkins, Stanley M., and Eric McKitrick. *The Age of Federalism.* New York: Oxford University Press, 1993.

Flexner, James Thomas. *George Washington.* 4 vols. Boston: Little, Brown, 1965–72.

Freeman, Douglas Southall. *George Washington: A Biography.* 7 vols. New York: Scribner, 1948–57.

Grizzard, Frank E. *George Washington: A Biographical Companion.* Santa Barbara, CA: ABC-CLIO, 2002.

Higginbotham, Don. *George Washington and the American Military Tradition.* Athens: University of Georgia Press, 1985.

Hofstra, Warren R. *George Washington and the Virginia Backcountry.* Madison, WI: Madison House, 1996.

Johnson, Gerald W. *Mount Vernon: The Story of a Shrine: An Account of the Rescue and Continuing Restoration of George Washington's Home by the Mount Vernon Ladies' Association.* Rev. ed. Mount Vernon, VA: Mount Vernon Ladies' Association, 1991.

Ketcham, Ralph. *Presidents Above Party: The First American Presidency, 1789-1829.* Chapel Hill: University of North Carolina Press, 1984.

Knollenberg, Bernhard. *George Washington: The Virginia Period, 1732–1775.* Durham, NC: Duke University Press, 1976.

Kwasny, Mark V. *Washington's Partisan War, 1775–1783.* Kent, OH: Kent State University Press, 1996.

Lewis, Thomas A. *For King and Country: George Washington. The Maturing of George Washington, 1748–1760.* New York: HarperCollins, 1993.

Longmore, Paul K. *The Invention of George Washington.* Berkeley: University of California Press, 1988.

McDonald, Forrest. *The Presidency of George Washington.* Lawrence: University Press of Kansas, 1994.

Phelps, Glenn A. *George Washington and American Constitutionalism.* Lawrence: University Press of Kansas, 1993.

Smith, Richard Norton. *Patriarch: George Washington and the New American Nation.* Boston: Houghton Mifflin Company, 1993.

Further Reading for Young People

Bruns, Roger. *George Washington.* New York: Chelsea House Publishers, 1987.

Chandra, Deborah, Madeleine Comara, and Brock Cole. *George Washington's Teeth.* New York: Farrar, Straus and Giroux, 2003.

Collins, Mary. *Mount Vernon.* New York: Children's Press, 1998.

Knight, James E. *The Winter at Valley Forge: Survival and Victory.* Mahwah, NJ: Troll Associates, 1982.

Marsh, Joan. *Martha Washington.* New York: Franklin Watts, 1993.

Old, Wendie C. *George Washington.* Springfield, NJ: Enslow Publishers, 1997.

Peacock, Louise. *Crossing the Delaware: A History in Many Voices.* New York: Atheneum, 1998.

Stefoff, Rebecca. *Washington.* Tarrytown, NY: Benchmark Books, 1999.

Places to Visit

The Colonial Williamsburg Foundation
P. O. Box 1776
Williamsburg, VA 23187
Phone: 757-229-1000

Federal Hall National Memorial
26 Wall Street (off Nassau Street)
New York, NY 10005
Phone: 212-825-6888

Fort Necessity National Battlefield
One Washington Parkway
Farmington, PA 15437
Phone: 724-329-5805

Fraunces Tavern Museum
54 Pearl Street
New York, NY 10004
Phone: 212-425-1776

George Washington's Ferry Farm
268 Kings Highway
Fredericksburg, VA 22405
Phone: 540-370-0732

George Washington Birthplace National Monument
1732 Popes Creek Road
Washington's Birthplace, VA 22443
Phone: 804-224-1732

Historic Fredericksburg Foundation, Inc.
604A William Street
Fredericksburg, VA 22401
Phone: 540-371-4504

Independence National Historical Park
143 South Third Street
Philadelphia, PA 19106
Phone: 215-597-8974

Mary Washington House
1200 Charles Street
Fredericksburg, VA 22401
Phone: 800-678-4748 or 540-373-1776

Morris-Jumel Museum
160th Street and Edgecomb Avenue
New York, NY 10032
Phone: 212-923-8008

Morristown National Historical Park
30 Washington Place
Morristown, NJ 07960
Phone: 973-539-2085

Mount Vernon
Mount Vernon Ladies' Association
P.O. Box 110
Mount Vernon, VA 22121
Phone: 703-780-2000

Valley Forge National Historical Park
P. O. Box 953
Valley Forge, PA 19482
Phone: 610-783-1077

Van Cortlandt Mansion
246th Street and Broadway
Bronx, NY 10471
Phone: 718-271-8981

Yorktown Victory Center
Route 1020
Yorktown, VA 23690
Phone: 757-253-4838

INDEX

Note: Page numbers in italics refer to photographs.

Adams, John, 43
American Revolution, 3, 26–37, *33*
Arnold, Benedict, 29
Articles of Confederation, 37

Braddock, General Edward, 18
Brooklyn, 27, *27*
Bruton Parish Church, *25*

Calvert, Eleanor (Nelly), 23
Colonial politics, 19, 23
Constitution, 37, *37*
Constitutional Convention, 37
Continental army, 3, 25, 26, *26*, 30
Continental Congress, 25, 29, 42
Conway Cabal, 29
Cornwallis, General Charles, 33
Couder, Louis-Charles Auguste, *33*
Custis, Daniel Parke, 20, 21
Custis, Eleanor Parke (Nelly), 26, 35, *35*
Custis, George Washington Parke, 35, *35*
Custis, John Parke (Jacky), 21, *21*, 23, 26, 33, *35*
Custis, Martha (Patsy), 21, *21*, 23

Dinwiddie, Governor Robert, 13

Fairfax family, 9
Federal government, 40, *41*, 43
Federal Hall, 38, *39*
Ferry Farm, 5, *6*, *7*, 9
Foreign policy, 39, 41, 43
Fort Duquesne, *14*, 15, 16, 18, *19*
Fort Le Boeuf, 13
Fort Necessity, 16, *16*, 17, *17*
France, *12*, 13, 33, 41
Fraunces Tavern, *42*, 43
Fredericksburg, Virginia, 5, *7*, *8*, 9
French and Indian War, 15–25
French Revolution, 41
Fry, Colonel, 15, 16

Gates, Horatio, 29
Great Britain, 13, 15, 25, 41
    troops in American Revolution, 27, *27*, 29, 30
Greene, Nathaniel, 33

Hamilton, Alexander/Hamiltonians, 40, *41*
Hawthorne, Nathaniel, 5
Hessians, 29

Individual rights, 40, *40*

Jay's Treaty, 41
Jefferson, Thomas/Jeffersonians, 7, 25, 40, *40*, 41

Kenmore Plantation, *10*

LaFayette, Marquis de, 30
Lee, Henry, *45*
Leutze, Emanual, 29
Lewis, Colonel Fielding, *10*
Lewis, Lawrence, 35

Madison, James, 38
Military leadership, 13, 19, 31
Morgan, Daniel, 33
Mount Vernon, 5, 9, 11, *11*, 20, *20*, 23, 26, *34*, *35*, 37, 44
    Washington buried at, *45*
    Washington's improvements at, 36, *36*

New York City, 27, 38, *39*, *42*, 43

Old Braddock Road, *18*

Philadelphia, 29
Political party system, 40, 43
Pope's Creek, 3, *3*, *4*
Potomac River, *4*, 5, *20*, 36
Presidency, 3, 37, *37*, 38–42
    accomplishments, 43
    left office, 43
    reelected, 41

Saratoga, New York, 29
Siege of Yorktown (painting), *33*
Slaves, freed, 45
States, independence for, 40, *40*
Stearns, Junius Brutus, *21*
Steuben, Baron von, 30

Thomas, Lord Fairfax, 10

United States, 3, 37, 41, 43

Valley Forge, 30, *30*, *31*
Virginia House of Burgesses, *22*, 23
Washington, Augustine (father), 3, *5*, 7, 9
Washington, Augustine Jr. (half-brother), 3
Washington, Betty (sister), 5, 10
Washington, George
    birth of, 3
    commander and chief of Continental army, 3, 25, 26, *26*, 29, 33
    death of, 44, *44*, 45
    early years, 3–14
    Farewell Address, *42*, 43
    horseman, 7
    illnesses, 18, 27
    later years, 43–45
    as leader, 3, 13, 19, 31
    marriage, 20-21, *21*, 44
    military career, 13, 15, 16, 17, 18–19, 25, 29, 30
    myths about, 5
    surveyor, 10, *10*
Washington, John (great-grandfather), *5*
Washington, Lawrence (grandfather), *5*
Washington, Lawrence (half-brother), 3, 9, 11, *11*
Washington, Martha Dandridge Custis (wife), 20-21, *21*, 23, 26, 27, 35, 44
    death of, 45
Washington, Mary Bell (mother), 3, *8*, 9, 10
Washington, Mildred (sister), 7
Washington Crossing the Delaware (painting), *28–29*
Weems, Parson, 5
Williamsburg, Virginia, 13, 23, *23*
    Governor's Palace, *22*

Yorktown, *32*

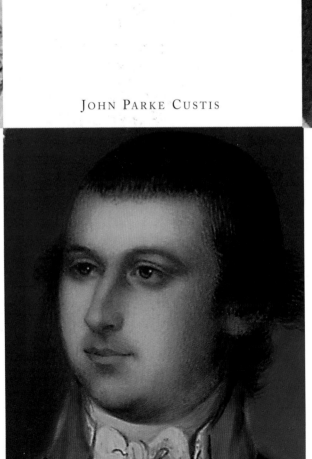

JOHN PARKE CUSTIS

MARTHA WASHINGTON

MARTHA PARKE CUSTIS